Patrick J. O'Connor

Some Guides to the Irish Scene

Irish Landscape Series no. 2

Oireacht na Mumhan Books

Published in Ireland by
Oireacht na Mumhan Books
Coolanoran
Newcastle West
Co. Limerick

Printed by Litho Press Co., Midleton, Co. Cork.

For John

kind of people we are, and were, and will be soon. Viewed in this way, the landscape is our unwitting autobiography. It reflects our tastes, our values, our ideals, our prejudices, even our fears, in clear tangible form. There are no secrets in the landscape; it is as open as an honest human face. P. Vidal de la Blache, the great French geographer, has said it well : 'the landscape is a medal struck in the image of its people.' Our cultural blots are there and so are our triumphs; but above all, our ordinary day-to-day qualities are displayed for anyone who has eyes to see them and a mind to take them in.

The ingredients of the landscape - fields, farms, houses, roads, cities etc. - represent an enormous investment of money, time and commitment. This being the case, people will not normally change the character of landscape unless they are under heavy pressure to do so. Therefore a major change in the look of the cultural landscape is likely to be reflected in a corresponding change in the culture of its makers. Take, for example, the changeover from rural to urban living which has accelerated markedly since *circa* 1950. In 1971, for the first time in Irish history, more than half the total population lived in centres with a threshold of 1500 persons or more, and both the Dublin and Belfast metropolitan regions accounted for about one-third of the populations of their respective jurisdictions.

Above all, in Dublin and its environs, we may focus upon the transformation of landscape. In the early 1940s the built-up area did not extend appreciably beyond the canal ring, but it has since engulfed outlying villages and the open countryside, and has extended greatly the range of urban and suburban tracts to the north and south, and more recently to the west. The physical city has more than doubled its area in a matter of decades, radiating out along the arterial roads and their interconnections, creating a new suburban world of housing, industrial estates, roads, shops, churches, schools etc., and representing an immense investment of time, money, and emotions. There is no slackening in the rate of growth. As one stern and steadfast critic puts it : 'the capital continues to expand at an alarming rate, sucking the life-blood out of the countryside, like an insatiable vampire. Is there nobody who will shout stop?' [6] In the process the urban-rural fringe has become increasingly blurred and so far there is no stopping Dublin's voracious appetite which continues to eat up land at the fringes at the rate of some 1,000 acres annually.[7] A really major change has occurred in the look of the capital's cultural landscape over the past fifty years or so. Indeed so thorough has been the metamorphosis that a major change in our national culture could only have been occurring at the same time.

And yet, it has all been a rather quiet affair which has unfolded in bits and pieces on the escalating fringe of the capital city. It is almost as if the great suburban sprawl has managed to creep into our consciousness by stealth, sometime after it had already assumed concrete form in the land. Everything has happened so fast. Many of us have seen it happen and have been participant - if passive - observers of the making of the new estates that make up the new suburbs.

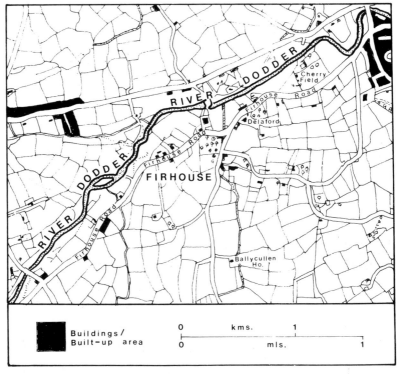

Fig. 2.1. Firhouse *circa* 1971 - a quiet road, gracious houses, green fields, wooded surrounds, a country pub or two —— a whole massy accretion that had been centuries in the making

Thinking about suburban Dublin now, I take 1971 as a baseline when with little on my mind, I was traversing the Firhouse Road to play pitch-and-putt in Bohernabreena. This was then countryside Dublin - a quiet road, gracious houses, green fields, wooded surrounds, a country pub or two - a whole massy accretion that had been centuries in the making. Five years later, I was back again in Firhouse with a wife and young daughter, to rent a house in a brand new estate. A large slice of

10

country had been transformed. Already Woodlawn Park estate was in place and maturing, and it had just been joined by Tymon Heights to affirm the grip of three-bedroomed, semi-detached suburbia over retreating farmland. Nearby in open space, pegs driven into the ground signalled the imminence of further development. It would take only a few days with the heavy machinery to sweep away a landscape whose forms had accrued for centuries, and at the same time mark out its replacement. Afterwards we monitored the new estate in progress, little thinking that some few months later we would join the ranks of newly weds and first-time buyers, and go to Carrigwood to a home of our own. We had seen, literally unfolding before our eyes, the sharp transition from old humanised landscape to new rational setting.[8] All of it had been induced, here as elsewhere, by one of the great psychological drives of our time - the quest for suburban living.

Plate 2.1. Shorn lawns, cars in driveways, children romping— the Carrigwood estate in Firhouse *circa* 1980

When the Carrigwood estate was completed in 1977/8, some 1,500 units in all had been built at Firhouse by the same developer, using only two variants of the basic three-bedroom, semi-detached house. All the usual charges of blandness and uniformity may be levelled at this rapidly built environment, but at the same time it would be churlish not to acknowledge the focusing of neighbourhoods around a central hub, the infill of houses around U shaped cul-de-sacs, and the provision of

11

adequate open space, including a large park. The hub evolved with great alacrity. To start, there was the shell of an aborted commercial enterprise, soon to be transformed into a shopping precinct by the entrepreneur, Albert Gubay. Alongside it, the church of a newly constituted parish duly took its place, and across the road two presbyteries and a school completed the early ensemble at the centre of a new community. At the edge, a sign on the Firhouse Road which issued a welcome to the amorphous concept of Tallaght New Town failed to last long enough for the workers who had erected it to finish their drinks in the Firhouse Inn. For this was already a self-conscious community, anxious to promote the concrete forms of its own identity, and capable of instant resort to the defence of its boundaries. This was the new suburban order maturing in minds and in the landscape within short years of its inception. It was proclaimed by shorn lawns and fluttering clothes lines; by cars in driveways, music blaring, children romping, people coming and people going.

Fig. 2.2. Firhouse *circa* 1981, at which time the new suburban order was maturing in minds and in the landscape within short years of its inception

12

Leaving Firhouse in 1981, I could look back over a decade of knowing an area which had experienced the change from quiet countryside to fully fledged suburb. The same process - often throwing up far more spectacular examples - was occurring at the same time right around the perimeter of the capital. Owner-occupied suburbs at the edge became spatially dominant among Dublin's social areas, [9] and at a time of ever increasing traffic the spread of the city began to pose formidable problems. These have since intensified. Indeed some measure of their immensity may be gauged from the kind of detailed changes that are needed to complete the Western Bypass motorway around the city by 1995.[10] National and metropolitan needs, as these are perceived, ensure that change is heaped upon change in and around Dublin. A child once saw a scratching post in the form of a cross in a field in Firhouse and exclaimed 'that's where the cows say their prayers!' The next day that image of bucolic innocence was gone forever.

Looking beyond the suburban rim, change in the landscape is also a powerful theme which has in large part been shaped by Dublin's spillover effects. Long established towns and villages within commuting range have all seen the addition of substantial housing developments in recent years. Such developments may be observed in a broad crescent around the capital extending roughly from Greystones in Co. Wicklow to Balbriggan in north Co. Dublin. These present all the appearance of a gravity model, with some of the largest concentrations found alongside settlements which are fast becoming part of the sprawling metropolis such as Bray, Lucan, Mulhuddart, Swords and Malahide. The preferred settlement strategy for the year 2011 predicts an intensification of such trends. Ringing Dublin then may be massed settlements of the order of Donabate (population:56,000), Swords (100,000), Blanchardstown (125,000), Leixlip, Celbridge and Maynooth (67,000), Lucan and Clondalkin (105,000), Tallaght (which has already well exceeded the 90,000 projection set for it) and Bray (48,000).[11] Further away from the centre, many small service centres have seen more change in the past decade than they did in the previous century. Places like Clane and Kilcock in Co. Kildare, and Dunboyne and Dunshaughlin in Co. Meath have all seen the spread of the dormitory village grafted on to existing forms, having been sucked rapidly into the Dublin metropolitan region. In a matter of years Clane has been transformed from a very small rural service centre to a largely dormitory settlement. Kilcock and Dunboyne in the 1980s have both seen the accretion of large housing estates showing clear directional biases at Courtown Lawn and

Beechdale respectively, and swift change at Dunshaughlin was underlined *circa* 1986 by no less than half of its migrant families taking up occupancy over the previous two years.[12]

Outside of towns and villages and sprawling suburbs, the intensity of the drive for houses in the metropolitan rural region may be seen as another index of culture change. Here a radical transformation of the settlement pattern is under way. Expansion occurs beyond the urban fringe, on the edges of towns and villages and in rural areas accessible to them. Instead of the dispersed farmstead of the past serving its own suite of fields, the settlement pattern is now road-orientated, unconnected with farming, and showing a marked tendency towards ribbon development in desirable areas. The Kilcloone area, reposing peacefully in the pasturelands of south Meath, illustrates the process well, having seen a rash of new house building to ribbon its roads since *circa* 1970.[13] This is by way of response to Dublin-generated pressure and to the demand for houses within commuting range of the capital. Depending upon site availability and other variables, the socially mobile resort eagerly to areas like Kilcloone where they can avail of urban levels of living in more tranquil surroundings. At worst, pressure upon roadside land may lead to extreme cases of ribbon development. Still there is no stopping the apportionment of half-acre plots or of the fashionable rural living that leads to it. In the late twentieth century the capital of a new Ireland for the first time pressures that of an old, as the approach roads to Tara show. It is all there in the landscape. We need only to look, put the questions, and reflect. Then we may feel the change.

Its measure is such that, to a far greater extent than any other European capital, Dublin and its region dominates the Republic of Ireland. This is spectacularly at odds with the older modes of Irish life and their mosaic of landscape expressions, and betokens some of the worst excesses of state centralism to be found anywhere in the world. It yields at the centre a city of 'paralysis', which is already remote from the images of Joycean stasis,[14] and which needs as a matter of urgency an end to the tyranny of traffic and the commencement of large-scale renewal and revitalisation. At one end of the spectrum, we may point to the 'centre of paralysis', chock-full by day and empty by night; at the other, there is the world of the rural backwater, drained at all times of most, if not all, of its energies. These are the cultural polarities that have come to mark Irish life as changing states of mind took form in the land. On the one side, there is the allure of the city; on the other, the repudiation of the countryside, and it is to the consequences of the latter that we will now turn.

14

For the cold facts of landscapes drained of their people, it is an easy matter to invoke such criteria as population decline, settlement desertion and low population densities. What has been lost, however, is a world buried in the backcountry with its own joys and sorrows, its own patterns and confusions, and all of it now more completely vanished than ancient Greece or Rome. It may take a poet to see through to this and when, for example, Montague surveys slopes strewn with cabins that have been deserted in his lifetime he transmutes them into the 'shards of a lost culture.'[15] *Beyond the Pale* and out in the realm of the midlands, Clarke finds scarcely a living soul upon the roads as 'both young and old hasten to quit the dung,' while all around him the tell-tale symptoms of neglect show in the 'thistle blow of fields once measured by buckshot.' [16] Up in a favoured locale, Hewitt paces

Plate 2.2. Glenariff, Co. Antrim, where life drains 'surely down the tree-dark glen'

lanes and takes in the change from homesteads to *wallsteads,* from playing children to flourishing nettles, and he contemplates the passing of the old men - shepherd, scythesman, blacksmith, carpenter - whose skills once tamed a landscape and whose disappearance coincides with life draining 'surely down the tree-dark glen.'[17] Filled with feeling and meaning, the poets are able to distil the essence of culture change as it is reflected to them in the landscape.

Others are able to do it too, and for an early and telling example, we may call upon one of the most percipient of our landscape readers, the writer, Sean O'Faolain. In his short story, *A broken world*, the land is portrayed as 'mountain bog, reclaimed by much labour, but always badly drained,' and emigration has depleted the population. 'The country is full of ruins —- scores on scores, with, maybe, a tree growing out of the hearth, and the marks of the ridges they ploughed, still there, now smooth with grass.'[18] This is no longer a sustaining landscape. Rather it has sank into sharp decline following upon the vanished social order of landlordism which, although unjust, maintained at least a measure of equilibrium. Later on in the 1960s, the

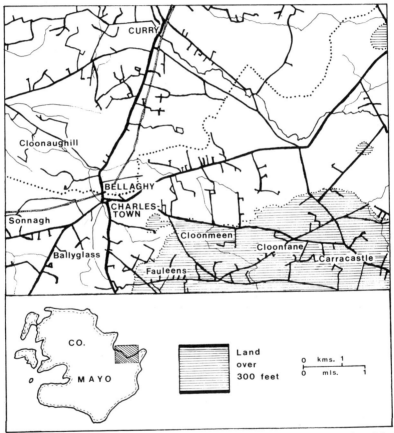

Fig. 2.3. Townlands around Charlestown, Co. Mayo, where Healy chronicled the themes of loneliness and emptiness in the 1960s

desiccation is such that it moves an impassioned commentator to see death writ large across the landscape of his native Mayo. Healy chronicles the themes of loneliness and emptiness in the townlands

16

around Charlestown and in the rush-soured fields there he sees an end to replenishment and the cumulative effects of out-migration.[19] Even on the margins of the good land, remarkable settlement expansion in the past may be thrown into sharp reversal by flight and by death. This is precisely what happened on Tipperary hill and bog edges where the geographer is on hand to record the meagre leavings.[20] Here Nolan enumerates lone trees, wild garlic and nettle clumps, defunct wells and blind cul-de-sacs as the only remaining tokens to attest to a once peopled landscape.

Given the extensive literature that now exists, it is not necessary to rehearse the causes of rural depopulation. For what has been lost to the backcountry, however, we may again summon up some discerning viewers of landscape and life. In *Ireland with Emily* written *circa* 1940, Betjeman tunes in to a rural order before the motor car. He captures the Sunday sounds 'booming down the bohreens' and in response knots of women 'move between the fields to Mass.'[21] Then on the sabbath, the Mass paths still conveyed a moving film of life, whether in the lush grasslands of Kildare or the thin, ash-loving pastures of Roscommon; whether in lake-strewn Westmeath or hill-rimmed Laois. At around the same time, Elizabeth Bowen looked out over the north east corner of Co. Cork, saw the same things, and committed her thoughts superbly to paper.[22] Her's was a countryside set to conceal its pattern of life. Everything combined to trick the eye - hedges, rivers, dips, creases, shelterbelts - and yet, as an aerial view would show, everything was interlinked by a complex of roads and boreens. Only on Sundays did the country reveal itself. Then everybody appeared as Mass going drew horses and traps from the backlanes, freewheeling cyclists from the mountain farms, and footsloggers balancing on stepping stones, legging it out over stiles, or tracking through plantations. At other times funerals, fairs, feiseanna, matches and races moved the people out and on weekday mornings the backroads rattled to the sound of creamery cans. Fine summer evenings brought gatherings around crossroad platforms where music was put under the feet of dancers, and when it was all over, the country rustled with the sound of people going home in darkness. In the days before the car and electricity, country life held many meanings, kept its own quiet rhythms, and penetrated deep into hidden backwaters. Its landscape conveyed only the illusion of emptiness, as Bowen and others have shown.

Things have since changed. There is nothing illusory about emptiness now as electrification, mechanisation and a new ideology combined to

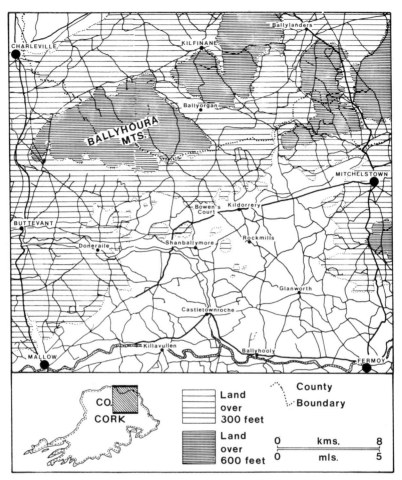

Fig. 2.4. Elizabeth Bowen's countryside where everything is portrayed as combining to trick the eye and yet, as the map shows, everything is interlinked by a complex of roads and boreens

suck the burden of labour out of farming, and push many of the uprooted on to the doorstep of an urban world. The theme of displacement is a compelling one. Outmigration and relocation have robbed the laneways and the backroads of their lifeblood; the settled countryside has contracted. Instead of the lateral prongs of the past probing deep into the backcountry and farmsteads set well in among their suite of fields, to-day's linear spread latches on to road frontages and yields a fresh rational order.

The country has lost its strength in depth. Walking the backlanes now

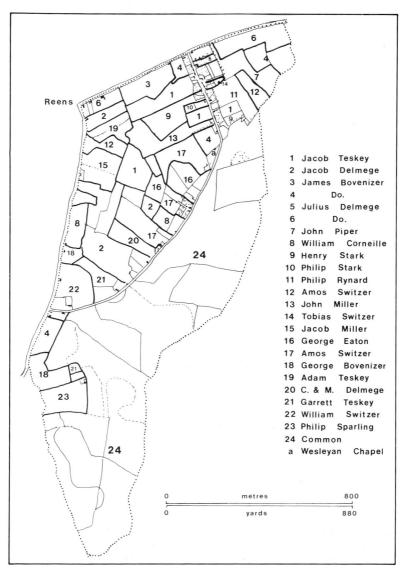

1 Jacob Teskey
2 Jacob Delmege
3 James Bovenizer
4 Do.
5 Julius Delmege
6 Do.
7 John Piper
8 William Corneille
9 Henry Stark
10 Philip Stark
11 Philip Rynard
12 Amos Switzer
13 John Miller
14 Tobias Switzer
15 Jacob Miller
16 George Eaton
17 Amos Switzer
18 George Bovenizer
19 Adam Teskey
20 C. & M. Delmege
21 Garrett Teskey
22 William Switzer
23 Philip Sparling
24 Common
a Wesleyan Chapel

| 0 | metres | 800 |
| 0 | yards | 880 |

Fig. 2.5. A Palatine micro-world - the townland of Killeheen in the parish of Kilscannell in west Co. Limerick *circa* 1850

is like being in a haunted land. As ever, there are few locales that anyone can really know and in seeking exemplification I find myself drawn to Irish Palatine country. [23] Specifically, I am drawn to Killeheen Lane - the old hearth of a parent colony - which stretches its curvilinear form to join the Rathkeale-Newcastle road on either side of Reens in west Co. Limerick. In living memory this was still the thread through a Palatine micro-world and clear confirmation of its standing at mid nineteenth century comes by way of the Griffith valuation map (fig. 2.5.). Killeheen was then a smallholders' domain - neat, ordered and vibrant - with linear open village, chapel/school, and holdings in severalty and in common. To-day the heart has been ripped out of it; its people have flown. In mid lane an old Bovenizer home stands abandoned and forlorn. Nearby the scant remains of a Delmege farm represent another stage in the same sad process of dissolution. In other cases, including the chapel, only the foundations may be traced. Fields and gardens, once lovingly tended, have reverted to semi-rough pasture. A Palatine farming presence has diminished to the lone personage of John Teskey Sr., whom one may meet aboard his tractor symbolically filling the lane. When he stops to talk, he draws on 280 years of occupancy in a little known townland, and on the rich tapestry of its life and landscape. Everything worthwhile resides in the past. The present is thin and the future bleak. Yet there is humour in the Teskey eye and banter in his voice.

A fox's brush picked up fleetingly in the car headlights in a backlane after nightfall symbolises for me a dissolving way of life. But that same vixen or her cub may go on to become a predator on the edge of the hungry city. The old dialectic of the country and the city goes on in Irish life, and in trying to sort out what it all means in a cultural context, we are obliged to read the landscape for really telling clues.

Seeing Things

We learn to see a thing by learning to describe it [24]

The landscape is inseparable from what goes on in it, and from the lives of the people who inhabit it [25]

Nearly all items in our vernacular landscape reflect culture in some way. Whether in the outreach of the country or the heart of the city makes no difference. There are almost no exceptions. The landscape may therefore be seen as a great repository of information relating to the kind of people we are, were, or will be. However, it is no easy matter to select from or determine the significance of the ordinary things that lie before our eyes. When we distil and evaluate our cumulative observations of a landscape, value judgements are involved at every turn. Moreover, the relationship between what we see and what we know is never settled. In the act of describing things we are discovering them and investing them with meaning. We are seeing beyond mere sighting; we are going beyond description.

Once on a February evening when driving home on the road that follows the Suir between Carrick and Clonmel, I was confronted by the vision of a hill-top graveyard delineated and illuminated by the light of a low sun. From nowhere this radiant green knoll lit up before my eyes and diminished everything else in sight into a backdrop of russet brown. It was a rare moment of brimming. For it served to transport me onto intimations of another world as well as to ponder the possible significance of the graveyard as an item in our own cultural landscape. The realisation that we live in an island full of funerary traces was by no means a new one but that sublime image, caught momentarily, triggered meditation on to the plane of afterlife and the intertwining themes of people, time and mortality. Contemplation of life and death came bounding into mind because here was a focus in the landscape that stood awhile for all foci.

Consider then the graveyard. It is a type of landscape. Its ill-kept state is frequently decried, but it can also be appraised for its religious and aesthetic qualities. People visit it for a variety of reasons : a relative or a famous person is buried there, or it acts as a local mecca on an appointed day. People may be drawn to it casually. The graveyard has a strange appeal. Its ambience induces a state of mind and this in turn affects perception.

Thinking about the old graveyard at Church Island in Lough Beg, the remembering Heaney sees it shoulder-high with meadowsweet and cow parsley, and shadowed with yew trees. Those sturdy yews fetched him back to the world of medieval archery, to bows made of yew, and to places like Agincourt and Crécy. [26] However, for a boy to cut a bough in that silent compound would have been tantamount to an act of treachery. Everything within its precincts was inviolate. Another northern poet steps 'clean out of Europe into peace' when in the townland of Kilmore in north Armagh he is drawn first and foremost to the old churchyard there.[27] Like Church Island, it too has Early Christian associations. But it is the tug of his planter ancestry that draws Hewitt to this place where the tombstones testify to the strength of his maternal links with the heart of apple country. Here in a churchyard in a 'townland of peace,' he finds solace, strength and a sense of personal renewal. Kennelly on the other hand finds a

Plate 2.3. A communal afterworld - the old parish centre of Aghavallen near
Ballylongford in north Co. Kerry, to which Kennelly, the poet,
resorts

distinctly communal dimension when he resorts to the old parish centre
of Aghavallen near his home in Ballylongford in north Co. Kerry. He
is struck by ' neighbours' names on stained slabs - / Johanna Enright,
Margaret Hayes, / Bart O'Sullivan, Naylus Connor /,'[28] and he
postulates a surname landscape with at least four centuries of
continuity. Moreover, the same family names are still around to-day to
take up 'the living challenge of the fields.' At the heart of O'Connor
Kerry country, tap roots strike deep into a Gaelic past and the poet is
able to identify a seamless community of the living and the dead.

The geographer brings other perspectives to bear. Looking at the old
parish centre of Shanrahan near Clogheen in south west Tipperary,
Smyth is struck by the motif of core and periphery to be found in the
disposition of its grave markers.[29] As in life itself, the landscape of
afterlife upholds a hierarchical order which ranges from ostentation to
anonymity. In Shanrahan the two central monuments commemorate
the local landlord lineage of O'Callaghan and the heroic personage of
Fr. Nicholas Sheehy, who was hanged in Clonmel in 1766. Wealth and
fame claim remembrance at the centre : poverty in contrast sinks into
oblivion at the edge. Yet, as Smyth points out, all the ground is sacred,
since this is the immemorial burial place for people locally. As such, it
represents a focal point in the landscape. Competitive and bonding
impulses find expression there and it links into other worlds where

ancestors reside. Shanrahan can never be seen therefore as a mere ruin. Rather it is, as Smyth claims, 'a place invested with the symbols of the identity of many competing families and one enduring community.'[30]

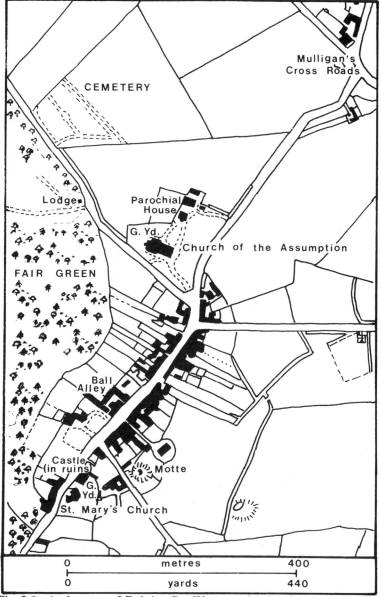

Fig. 2.6. A close-up of Delvin, Co. Westmeath, showing *inter alia* the cemetery and the handball alley

Enough has been adduced to suggest that old graveyards with weathered stone gables and scatter of lichen-encrusted gravestones rank among the most evocative features of the Irish landscape. This is not to infer, however, that the appeal of new cemeteries is in any way diminished by comparison. On the contrary, there is every bit as much to engage the eye and the mind, and in focusing upon a particular setting, I find myself drawn to the cemetery that lies alongside the Church of the Assumption in Delvin, Co. Westmeath. This is the enduring symbol of my mother's country; it is here that our people are buried. Throughout most of my childhood it acted as a focus in the annual cycle of family life, as our summer holidays at Rosmead near Delvin were always chosen to coincide with a day in August, known locally as 'Cemetery Sunday.' For as long as counted this was the great gathering day of the parish and in my own mind's eye it goes back to a time when the shunting of a steam engine at Newcastle West railway station signalled the start of a long day's journey to the midlands.

In the week before the appointed day a clean-up of the cemetery grew in intensity as time grew shorter. Often I would go there with my uncle, ostensibly to help with the weeding, but more likely to be drawn into games with my brother. The child looks around in the cemetery and sees the perfect landscape for variants of the game of hide-and-seek. Then the fun takes over. Later it might yield to minute observations of colonies of crawling ants, not to mention the stings they inflicted, and stories of their prodigious strength would stretch out a child's imagination. All the while the work went on amid quiet exchanges, and for those who left no immediate relatives, close ties of neighbourliness or more distant ties of kinship often ensured that their graves too came within the remit of the annual clean-up. At the weekend the cemetery showed off its shining face. All this was utterly at variance with anything I had known among the unkempt graveyards of west Limerick and added to the allure of Delvin.

Cemetery Sunday came. Preparations still went on apace. Flowers were plucked and wreaths made, and from about noon onwards floral tributes to a remembered people began to bedeck the graves. A strong competitive drive underpinned this day set aside for the living as well as for the dead. It showed in the preparatory work beforehand and it showed on the day in the wreaths of gladioli and dahlias and assortments of autumn flowers. Everything predisposed towards furnishing a splendid commemorative setting, as the people gathered and the priest and his acolytes appeared for the afternoon ceremony. All the spaces seemed to fill in around the central monument. Here the priest stood before the grave of his predecessors and led the prayers. Everyone remembered their own. They were asked to pray for all and they did so fervently. Layers of meaning inhered in the landscape : knots of kneeling people forged a community of the living, evoked a sense of communion between the living and the dead, and fused with the presence of an all-embracing God. Afterwards people would comment on how the cemetery had filled up since last year. They would renew old acquaintances and inquire after absent friends. Then the great gathering of the parish dispersed into pubs and homes. Next year the landscape of afterlife would draw them all together again!

Plate 2.4. A rapidly evolving commemorative field - Calvary Cemetery, Newcastle West, Co. Limerick

Whether crowded or quiet, the cemetery exerts its curious appeal over the human psyche.[31] This in turn affects how the eye sees it. Another critical factor is one's stage in the life cycle, and from the crowded days of remembrance in Delvin in the 1950s, I now find myself making solitary visits to the cemetery in Newcastle West, where my father is buried. Like many of the new cemeteries, this has been a rapidly evolving commemorative field since its origin in the early 1970s. The name of the 'first man to go in there' is still well recollected, and from the line-up of memorials placed in rows running upslope, a remarkably close pattern of leavetaking may be reconstructed. This is a landscape shot through with the signs of mortality. Here a whole generation, once known in the prime of life, has come to repose. The visitor wanders about slowly between the graves, looking at the headstones; reading the names, and being drawn to some of them. All kinds of signal are set off by memorials which recall a father, an aunt, a neighbour, a teacher, a friend —! Meanings hold fast; feelings flow. Then the visitor who came alone, and who alone stands upright, goes away again. There are other things to see and think about.

Let us turn therefore from the landscape of afterlife, and from among the array of features observed out-of-doors, consider an ordinary item from the landscape of play. This is the handball alley - an architectural feature peculiar to Ireland - which has passed almost without notice in the literature.[32] Like many ordinary things it crept surreptitiously on to the scene, often finding its earliest expression on the disreputable or unsavoury rims of towns and villages in the second half of the nineteenth century. It is typically associated with fair green settings where it served the everyday needs of the people in combination with such items as a chapel, a school, a smithy, a barrack, a pound and a dispensary. Some of the best examples come from the midlands, from where Kilbeggan in Co. Westmeath furnishes perhaps the finest instance of a ball alley set in a fair green milieu. Elsewhere its characteristic standing at or beyond the edge of settlement is well attested in places as diverse as Broadford, Co. Limerick, Ballingarry in north Co. Tipperary and Barna, Co. Galway. Within the precincts of University College, Galway, the ball alley upholds its customary peripheral location, so much so that it lured in the travellers to play, and in a short time they proceeded to make their own of it. Indeed the alley is often seen as serving the casual needs of marginalised or disaffected youths. It may therefore be consigned to the margins of the mind, a status which accords with the random nature of its appearance or disappearance. Often as not, ball alleys are adaptations of existing buildings : wherever a high blank wall presents itself, it invites the addition or adaptation of two side-walls to make a suitable structure. The provision of a back-wall is an optional extra.

Yet the handball alley can count and has counted both as a landscape feature and a type of landscape in its own right. Healy, for example, sees in it an evocation of his native Charlestown.[33] Whereas before World War 2 the ball alley facilitated many a hectic tussle on a Sunday afternoon, later its growing silence connoted young men on the move with their cardboard suitcases. The scourge of emigration hit home hard in Charlestown. Heroes vanished. Familiar alley sounds went into abeyance, only to be revived sporadically, and then go dead again. In the end it all came down to one man and to the test of individual worth. This was a man who in his youth could 'mark a circle of six

Plate 2.5. The handball alley, scene of many a hectic tussle on a Sunday afternoon

inches on the alley floor and then toss a round-the-house ball to touch all four walls and hop at the end in the circle.'[34] He too had succumbed to the plague of out-migration but came back home eventually. The deserted ball alley beckoned once again. Soon the town grew accustomed to this solitary figure and from the sounds he made of an evening came a crop of three All-Ireland medals. The last of Healy's heroes, an anachronism in his middle years, had yielded the fruit of all his youthful promise in the walled arena.

From this superb portrayal of one man's triumph, it is but a short step to the remembrance of stirring contests in the handball alley. Delvin in the 50s again claims the part of prominence, by virtue of the annual tournament held there on Lady Day, August 15. This was a big occasion locally and the day's proceedings were spiced with the prospect of inter-county competition. Word of the various arrivals spread like wildfire through the stepped arena. Below in the theatre of action the preliminary rounds were contested by representatives from as many as a dozen counties. Walls reverberated to the sounds of the half-solid, the calls of players and the dissonance induced by competition. Above, the scorekeeper, known to all and sundry as 'Micky the Taste', issued his pronouncements. All around the crowd reacted with groans, with cheers, and with stunning approbation upon delivery of the masterstroke of handball - a dead butt hit hard and true. Overhead the

Plate 2.6. The two local lads, Geelan (right) and Mullan, who beat the Mayo
lads in an enthralling semi-final in Delvin on August 15, 1959, with
their trainer, Paddy O'Shaughnessy

day invariably threatened showers, and should rain come, it would take
a frenzy of mopping up before play could resume. One year two local
lads representing the home county beat the Mayo lads in an enthralling
semi-final. They were no match, however, for the wily men of Louth.
Still no matter : for weeks afterwards the alley cracked with sounds
made in the manner of heroes.

From the landscape of play we will proceed to that of projected home
living. This will serve to underline the eclectic nature of the concept,
while also affording an opportunity to engage once again images of
common things that attract little notice in literature. In entering the
engagement, we are drawn by force of concentration back to the Dublin
metropolitan region and to the analysis of directories of new houses.
Specifically attention will be focussed upon 80 separate developments
which offered houses for sale at between £40,000 and £60,000 in the
first half of 1991.[35] Together these yielded a novel landscape and one
that was priced and packaged to attract the ordinary run of first-time
buyers. What are we to make of it ?

Certain salient features emerge straightaway. For one thing, most of
the names evoke a sense of urban retreats so embowered as to appear
rural. Here in the metropolitan region the rural-natural has undergone a
cultural transformation; it is re-presented. It is as if the bricks and

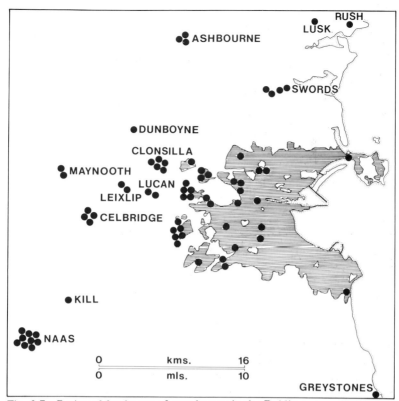

Fig. 2.7. Projected landscape of new homes in the Dublin metropolitan region containing units in the range of £40,000-£60,000, January - June, 1991

mortar are infused with the purity of the countryside.[36] Moreover, the proliferation of 'woods', 'brooks', 'parks' and 'dales' is symptomatic of a certain anti-urban tendency in modern thought that accords well with the notion of *rus in urbe*. In the popular imagination - to which, we must assume, these name elements are responsive - the landscape of new homes is projected as a sedately voluptuous locale. It comes packaged with a plant cover and a surface configuration that is ideally beautiful. Woodland or grassland or some park-like combination thereof prevails; its appeal is Edenic or pastoral. Let us examine therefore the particular items of flora and contour that contribute to such a perfected loveliness.

To start, this is a decidedly bosky domain in which sylvan elements or types of individual tree enter into the make-up of 26 of the 80 new place-names. *Wood, grove* and *forest* all put in an appearance in descending order of frequency and seductive names are fashioned out of Bramley Wood, Laverna Grove and River Forest. As for individual

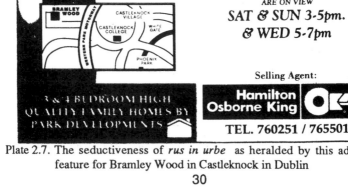

BRAMLEYWOOD

CARPENTERSTOWN ROAD, CASTLEKNOCK

"Be tempted by Dublin's Most Successful New Housing Development"

Bramley Wood is one of Dublins most successful new housing developments. It is built by Ireland's leading house builder - Park Developments, and offers a choice of five house styles in a prime location close to the new suburban rail station, the Western Park Motorway, bus routes and provides rapid access to the city centre in less than twenty minutes. It is adjacent to shopping centre, schools, collegesand the Phoenix Park.

Bramley Wood with its unique features is a superb investment .

FIVE FULLY FURNISHED SHOWHOUSES
ARE ON VIEW

SAT & SUN 3-5pm.
& WED 5-7pm

Selling Agent:

Hamilton Osborne King

TEL. 760251 / 765501

3 & 4 BEDROOM HIGH QUALITY FAMILY HOMES BY PARK DEVELOPMENTS

Plate 2.7. The seductiveness of *rus in urbe* as heralded by this advertising feature for Bramley Wood in Castleknock in Dublin

30

species, the noble oak leads the way with five occurrences. In part this may reflect the incidence of the genus *Quercus* in the countryside. But the oak also symbolises strength and endurance, and hence longevity; and the word *oak* carries no double meanings. Next in order the genus *Pinus* monopolises evergreen items, with *pine* registering three appearances. The stately elm also manages to recur, despite being bedevilled by disease in recent years. As for the rest, it is comprised of an amalgam of ash, beech, hazel, willow, whitethorn and cherry, and the most favoured compounds in this wooded realm include *brook, field* and *dale*.

No less emphatic is the range of elements referring to the pastoral world of parkland, meadow and lawn, and those which relate to the lie of the land. Taken together, these also number 26. *Park* is easily the most dominant element in this green - and by implication - grassy environment, in which the fern is the only other vegetative form to register a presence by name. Something of the same stability may be found in the vision of its surface configuration. This vision has been, and still is, of a land of rolling hills, replete with heights and downs and an occasional crest, punctuated by valleys and dales (but never a bottom or a hollow), and watered by rivers and brooks. There is no room evidently in this imaginative lexicon for prosaic or slightly vulgar terms. Sloping land seems to prevail everywhere in the absence of any references to level terrain. It is a land of visual orientation, almost always offering some striking feature to be viewed. Sometimes, the element *view* is itself incorporated. A prospect is promised, for example, of the Grand Canal at Kilmainham, of the harbour at Wicklow, of a wood at Celbridge, and of Binn Éadair at Sutton. Almost nothing about this landscape is distinctively Irish; Binn Éadair standing for Howth provides the solitary piece of linguistic evidence.

The only other major line of appeal in this domain of new houses is to historic and traditional values. In the Dublin metropolitan region as elsewhere in comparable situations in Britain and North America, there appears to be an imaginary conflation of past and present. The present is re-presented in relation to the past; the past is also appealed to as a dimension for future consumption.[37] All this appears perfectly congruent with the packaging of a rural-natural locale. The only settlement items to merit inclusion are *village, hamlet, priory* and *mill*, and the only land units to find recognition are *manor* and *court*. Collectively, these register a total of 20 occurrences. Thus we can establish that nine-tenths of the toponymic content of the landscape of £40,000-£60,000 houses falls into three broad categories which evoke images of the rural-natural order and of the past. To further enhance the vision of transposed rurality, we may add in the names of Stonebridge, Sunday's Well and Inismore.

This, then, is what the evidence of place-names reveals about the envisaged landscape of ordinary new homes. It is a land of rolling hills and fine prospects in which all the senses save the visual are numb. It is an evergreen, featuristic land of never varying climate where brooks and rivers flow, and trees and lawns flourish, without any trace of animal life. It is a place of great tranquillity and quietude; the only edifices and the only settlements are more at home in the countryside than anywhere else. The past matters solely for its more harmonious components which convey the sense of intimate settings, laden with quiet interaction potential, but at the same time capable of proclaiming exclusiveness. Concerning the inhabitants of this territory, our blurred legend has little to say about work and nothing at all about play. The vision is that of an ideal realm far removed from the workaday world. It would indeed be hard to imagine a greater contrast than that between the gritty actuality of landscape and life, as we know it, and the visual harmony suggested by our new onomastic evidence. But the names also create anticipations of the dream home in a world shaped by the self-authorship of participant observers. Which is the more real?

History Matters

History isn't handed down,
It's handed up —
History is in the bounce of a ball
In the flick of a skipping-rope [38]

Historical flavour now permeates even the most modern
aspects of life —- Events and landscapes from the past
become ever more like what we prefer the present to be [39]

In an island such as ours with a long and continuous record of human occupation, the cult of the past is an old story. Like any old story, however, it has undergone many a mutation over time, and none more so than that caused by the recent transition from rural to urban living.

By 1981, only one-third of the total population of Ireland, north and south, lived in the open countryside or in settlements with less than 250 inhabitants.[40] The kind of life change that has become an identity marker of modernising societies everywhere is thus well manifested here and it gathers pace as urbanising influences sweep the land. Nostalgia for the countryside and for rural ways, which is such a pervasive sentiment in Britain and North America, has already become well established. Similarly the growth of countryside concern in Ireland, as in Britain and North America, is largely a consequence of the accelerated pace of rural-urban migration. Fifty years ago a majority of the Irish were still country people; to-day they are drawn within the remit of urban settlements. The 'greening' of Dublin is the outstanding instance of this phenomenon. Thus most of our urbanites or their parents go straight back to the countryside for their immediate roots. This massive displacement over so short a span has intensified a commonly professed revulsion for urban settings and social institutions and has fed a longing for rural scenes. And issues concerning the appearance of the countryside - the retention or removal of earthworks and hedgerows, the design and layout of farm buildings, the planting of coniferous or deciduous trees, the preservation of small-scale variety of field and hedge, heath, copse, and covert against the demands of large-scale farming - are of the greatest interest to increasing numbers of townspeople.

Increasingly too, the countryside is being considered as our rightful heritage, to be preserved from modern encroachments. At the same time, we tend to overlook or to idealise the rural social fabric which is now much changed relative to that of a half a century ago and is in any case largely invisible. The urbanisation of rural life in Ireland as elsewhere may pass with little notice in the landscape.[41] Fewer and fewer people live the country life anymore and images of unchanging rurality, as conveyed *circa* 1940, now appear strange and incongruous.[42] Most rural dwellers nowadays, be they farmers or not, have similar tastes and enjoy comparable levels of living to their urban counterparts. However, as the open countryside grows emptier by the year, our remembrance of the rural world grows fonder. Its virtues are viewed as natural, moral and historic. Thus our image of the countryside tends more and more to reside in the realm of the past, and as we have already seen, images of transposed rurality may furnish us with the dominant *leitmotiv* for urban living. We could be accused therefore, as we have often been before, of living in the past.

Except that now things are different; change at an unprecedented rate means that the past can no longer be taken for granted. The more we

33

feel the need of it, the more we are obliged to recollect it, reinterpret it, even reinvent it. No longer is the museumised past a rare feature, to be viewed on special occasions in special situations where its content and meaning are carefully controlled. Rather, to judge from the recent proliferation of centres with a folk flavour and a local or regional accent, it is more and more a mirror held up to a vanished vernacular order. Increasingly enamoured of the ordinary past, we wish to see it re-presented. Let us look therefore at some of its museumised dimensions.

By the 1980s an impressive rate of museum dispersion had become evident throughout the island as a whole and the pattern had grown increasingly complex. At the top, regional centres which had blazed a pioneering trail, put on display large assemblages from the vernacular past. Three stand out prominently. These are the Ulster Folk and Transport Museum at Cultra Manor near Holywood in Co. Down, the Ulster-American Folk Park at Camphill near Omagh in Co. Tyrone, and Bunratty Folk Park near Shannon in Co. Clare. All encompass a past with which people of Irish birth or descent may readily identify.

Plate 2.8. Mediating between Old World and New, a ship and dockside gallery conveys a charged sense of the trials of earlier trans Atlantic migration at the Ulster-American Folk Park at Camphill near Omagh

At Cultra the focus is upon landscape and life in Ireland as it existed *circa* 1900. Irish dwellings of the time - both rural and urban - have been reconstructed, together with much of the attendant detail of folk and craft life. Here everything predisposes towards making the park seem as 'real' as possible, so that the visitor may feel drawn back into the atmosphere of a period within the scope of memory, when time apparently stood still. At Camphill, in contrast, the dynamic theme of Ulster-American emigration in the eighteenth and nineteenth centuries is expounded. In the re-presented landscape the visitor is able to move from the Old World to the New by taking in a blacksmith's forge, a weaver's cottage, a meeting house, a schoolhouse and original emigrant homesteads on the one side, and on the other a log cabin, a log barn, a corn crib, a smoke house, a spring house, and a Pennsylvania log farmhouse and garden. Mediating between the two, a ship and dockside gallery conveys a highly charged sense of the trails and trials of earlier trans Atlantic migration. In Bunratty as in Cultra the emphasis is on a welcoming Irish world in stasis. Here a representative sample of vernacular farmhouses from the region is dispersed throughout the park. In addition the rural ensemble includes a blacksmith's forge, a weaver's shed and a horizontal mill as well as the fringe settlement items of bothán scóir, fisherman's house and byre dwelling. Complementing all of this, a highly imaginative village street - featuring reconstructions of a post office, pawnbrokers, schoolhouse, craft shops, doctor's surgery, draper's shop, and a bar & hotel - seeks to recreate an inviting image of Ireland *circa* 1900, and as ever in such settings an attempt is made to reproduce a pleasing old world ambience. This is a place in which it is claimed that 'history comes alive.' [43]

Plate 2.9. A highly imaginative village street at Bunratty Folk Park which purports to re-present a vision of Ireland *circa* 1900

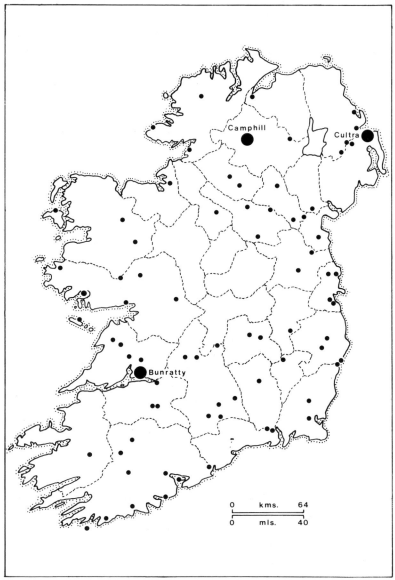

Fig. 2.8. Museums *circa* 1983 strongly committed to the re-presentation of vernacular items from the past

At local level too, attempts to revivify the ordinary past and re-present it may be observed in a wide variety of situations throughout the island by the time of first publication of a museums' guide in 1983.[44] At that time places designated as folk museums filled the largest generic category and examples might be drawn from locations as diverse as Knock, Co. Mayo; Toomevara, Co. Tipperary; Mullaghbawn near Forkhill, Co. Armagh; Crover near Mount Nugent, Co. Cavan; Glencolmcille, Co. Donegal; and Inniskeen, Co. Monaghan. To these might be added the Fethard Folk and Transport Museum which opened in 1983 and which has since gone from strength to strength as a focal point in south Co. Tipperary. At Tuam in Co. Galway and at Cookstown in Co. Tyrone the old landscape of milling had become successfully museumised, while at Mullinahone in Co. Tipperary and Johnstown Castle in Co. Wexford the themes that gather around threshing and the working horse were each redepicted. Sometimes on the threshold of the city, as in north Co. Dublin, for instance, an unmitigated appeal to nostalgia was evoked in the good old days exhibition at Rush and the Willie Monk's Museum at Lusk. On the other hand, the rugged insular world of the west came to be represented in centres such as Museum Árainn at Kilronan on Inishmore, the Achill Museum at Dugort, and Iarsmalann Chléire at Lios Ó Moine on Cape Clear.

Mediating between urban fringe and western isle there was a range of heritage, display and interpretative centres which were all of historical import, as well as a spread of town based museums which showed a similar commitment to re-presentation of vernacular items from the past (fig. 2.8.). In Co. Cork alone the towns of Clonakilty, Cobh, Kanturk, Kinsale, Macroom, Millstreet, and Youghal would merit enumeration on this account, and joining them elsewhere by 1983 were the towns of Lisburn and Larne in Co. Antrim, Carrickmacross in Co. Monaghan, Ballinamore in Co. Leitrim, Cahir, Roscrea and Nenagh in Co. Tipperary, and Ennis in Co. Clare. Also by this time the cult of personality had come to inspire awe and to count as part of the museumised landscape. Rebel, revolutionary, poet and statesman had all been gathered within the commemorative embrace and the humility of their homeplaces - as represented by the Dwyer-MacAllister cottage at Derrynamuck, Co. Wicklow; Patrick Pearse's cottage at Rosmuc, Co. Galway; Francis Ledwidge's cottage at Slane, Co. Meath; and the DeValera cottage at Bruree, Co. Limerick - became a matter of deep symbolic significance. Elsewhere, the incantatory power of the names of the founder of the Irish Christian Brothers, Ignatius Rice, and of the founder of the Land League, Michael Davitt, was invoked to re-collect their life and times at Waterford city and at Straide, Co. Mayo respectively.

City and county museums also came into their own. Drawing *inter alia* upon ordinary exhibits from the past, versions of the history of the cities of Dublin, Belfast, Cork, Limerick, Galway and Kilkenny had all found expression in prestigious centres by 1983. Sometimes particular display themes were developed. In Belfast's Ulster Museum, for example, industrial archaeology claimed the part of prominence in deference to the proud tradition of a city and a province; in Cork's Public Museum on the other hand, the re-presentation of butter-making and the Butter Market recalled the halcyon days when a city drew in the produce of a province. By this time too museum provision struck a responsive chord at county level and county museums had been established in Carlow, Cavan (Cootehill), Fermanagh (Enniskillen), Monaghan, Sligo, Tipperary (Clonmel) and Wexford (Enniscorthy). All exemplified a commitment to displaying the ordinary things of life; indeed Monaghan's prize-winning museum might be seen as an exemplar in the presentation of vernacular items from the past. More has been added to the network in recent years, including Down (Downpatrick), Kerry (Tralee) and Longford, and the commitment to the re-presentation of ordinary county history has deepened. At the Down Museum in Downpatrick, for instance, one of the most striking exhibits is a large-scale map which purports to show the surname landscape of the county. Such a map is rooted in the richest layerings of vernacular culture and calls to mind the county as a gathered entity shaped by lineages over time.

Plate 2.10. The Irish Palatine Heritage Centre, phase one of which nears completion at Rathkeale, Co. Limerick

All over Ireland a future for re-presenting ordinary things of the past seems reinforced with the further impressive spread of museum displays during the past decade. History is now being dealt with more and more on a small-h level; the master narrative is simply too large-scale and too abstract to carry the freight of identification. Local interests continue to seek and find expression, whether in Dungarvan or Donaghmore, Tullow or Tullaherin, Kilmacrennan or Kiltimagh. Minority interests too register their mark, whether in an expanded setting for the Quakers at Ballitore, Co. Kildare; or a new heritage centre for the Palatines at Rathkeale, Co. Limerick; or a museum for the Jews at Walworth Road in Dublin. Subjects such as famine and emigration which were formerly taboo, and which affected the broad mass of the population, are now deemed fit for re-presentation. The Great Famine, for example, finds local prominence in venues at Strokestown, Co. Roscommon and Louisburgh, Co. Mayo, while emigration features among the themes displayed in the windmill complex at Blennerville, Co. Kerry.

There is still a long way to go, however, in getting away from sanitised and carefully orchestrated versions of the past. Rarely, if ever, has the Irish museumised landscape dealt in a substantive way with death, starvation, sanitation, disease etc.[45] Representational modes still favour recorded history over the broader concept of geohistory. Idealised and picturesque views tend to prevail at the expense of properly authenticated settings. Displays frequently owe more to theatrical presentation than to the lives of the people they purport to represent. In short, our museums may tell us more about our attitude to the past than they do about the past for its own sake. To understand the re-presented objects, we must try to understand the people who made them in their cultural context, not ours. The past, as one distinguished geohistorian expounds at length, is a foreign country, where they do things differently.[46] In museums all over Ireland the challenge to be met therefore is one in which the consideration of history is paramount.

Our embrace of ordinary historical freight has certainly been impressive in recent decades. So has been the contemporaneous growth and development of local history, while fashion also ordains that we become more historically minded than ever before. The landscape now elicits a spate of commemorative responses, whether in a treaty city such as Limerick; or a walled town such as Athenry, Co. Galway; or an estate village such as Mountshannon, Co. Clare. Everywhere, it seems, there is some historical event waiting to be celebrated. Pageantry and re-enactment take to the stage and the land, and the past is accorded symbolic affirmation in words and slogans.

Historical outings are being organised on an ever-increasing scale; in the Antrim-Derry coastlands alone there is the prospect of guided summer tours surveying the 'historic glens of Antrim', the history and heritage of the Bann valley, Palmer's mill at Bushmills, the Moravian village of Gracehill, the Leslie Hill historic farm and park in Ballymoney, and the Causeway coast as it was envisioned by Charles Lever, the nineteenth century novelist.[47] History is also being extended; for instance, the major sustaining plank in the 'best of Belfast 1991' was an historical exhibition which purported to tell the story of the city from the Ice Age to the twentieth century. And the authority of the past is constantly being invoked for everything from architectural innovation to environmental conservation. Its influence remains to colour every landscape, action and ideal, and in trying to make sense of all, history - with a small-h - matters.

Notes and References

1. W. Stevens, *The collected poems of Wallace Stevens*, New York, 1981, 502.
2. P. Lewis, 'Axioms for reading the landscape : some guides to the American scene,' in D.W. Meinig (ed.), *The interpretation of ordinary landscapes*, New York, 1979, 11-12.
3. E. Munro, *Origins : American women artists*, New York, 1979, 78.
4. T.S. Eliot, *Four quartets*, London, 1979, 21.
5. P. Lewis, 1979, *op. cit.*, 15.
6. F. McDonald, 'News focus,' *Irish Times*, 19 January, 1983, 10.
7. NESC, 55, *Urbanisation : problems of growth and decay in Dublin*, Dublin, 1981, 234.
8. E. Relph, *Rational landscapes and humanistic geography*, London, 1981, 88-93.
9. NESC, 55, 1981, *op. cit.*, 103 ; J.E. Brady, 'Population change in Dublin 1981-86,' *Irish Geography* 21, 1, 1988, 41-4.
10. *Irish Times*, 20 May, 1991, 2 ; *Irish Independent*, 20 May, 1991, 17-33.
11. ERDO, *Eastern Region settlement strategy 2011*, Dublin, 1985, 257.
12. D.A. Gillmor, 'An investigation of villages in the Republic of Ireland,' *Irish Geography* 21, 2, 1988, 58.
13. P.J. Duffy, 'Planning problems in the countryside,' in P. Breathnach and M.E. Cawley (eds.), *Change and development in rural Ireland*, Maynooth, 1986, 62-3.
14. My intention,' James Joyce said, ' was to write a chapter in the moral history of my country, and I chose Dublin for the scene because that city seemed to me the centre of paralysis.'
15. J. Montague, *The rough field*, Mountrath, 1984, 34.
16. A. Clarke, *Collected poems*, Dublin, 1974, 289.
17. J. Hewitt, *Loose ends*, Belfast, 1983, 26.
18. S. O'Faolain, *The collected stories of Sean O'Faolain*, Boston, 1983, 166.
19. J. Healy, *The death of an Irish town*, Cork, 1968, 86.
20. W. Nolan, ' Patterns of living in county Tipperary from 1770 to 1850,' in W. Nolan (ed.), *Tipperary : history and society*, Dublin, 1985, 316.
21. J. Betjeman, *Collected poems*, London, 1979, 121.
22. E. Bowen, *Bowen's Court*, London, 1942, 2-3.
23. Although such country may be accounted exotic in terms of its ethnic content, in all other respects it typifies the well known process of loss and desertion. See, P.J. O'Connor, *People make places : the story of the Irish Palatines*, Newcastle West, 1989, espec. pp 189-209.
24. R. Williams, *The long revolution*, London, 1961, 39.
25. N.J. Parezo et. al., ' The mind's road,' in V. Norwood and J. Monk (eds.), *The desert is no lady : southwestern landscapes in women's writing and art*, New Haven, 1987, 167.

26. S. Heaney, *Preoccupations : selected prose 1968-1978,* London, 1978, 19.

27. J. Hewitt, *Freehold and other poems,* Belfast, 1986, 12-13.

28. B. Kennelly, *Dream of a black fox,* Dublin, 1968, 27.

29. W.J. Smyth, ' Explorations of place,' in J. Lee (ed.), *Ireland : towards a sense of place,* Cork, 1985, 6.

30. *Ibid.,* 6.

31. E. Canetti, *Crowds and power,* Harmondsworth, 1973, 321-2.

32. M. Craig, *The architecture of Ireland,* London, 1982, 17.

33. J. Healy, 1968, *op. cit.,* 39-42.

34. *Ibid.,* 40.

35. *Irish Independent Property Supplement,* January 4 - July 5, 1991. This supplement published on Fridays contains the most comprehensive and easily available listing of new houses for sale in the Dublin metropolitan region. It also contains extensive advertising features.

36. K. Whelan, ' Placename change : an index of value systems in transition,' *Sinsear* 1, 1979, 48.

37. J. Eyles, ' Housing advertisements as signs : locality creation and meaning systems,' *Geografiska Annaler* 69 B, 1987, 103.

38. W.R. Rodgers, quoted in V. Payne, ' Taking Ireland's history off the streets,' *Observer Magazine,* 2 December, 1979, 75.

39. D. Lowenthal, ' The bicentennial landscape : a mirror held up to the past,' *The Geographical Review* 67, 3, 1977, 257.

40. A.A. Horner, ' Rural population change in Ireland,' in P. Breathnach and M.E. Cawley (eds.), 1986, *op. cit.,* 34-47.

41. See my review of M.J. Shiel's, *The quiet revolution : the electrification of rural Ireland 1946-1976,* Dublin, 1984, in *Irish Geography* 18, 1985, 82-3.

42. C.M. Arensberg and S.T. Kimball, *Family and community in Ireland,* Cambridge, Massachusetts, 1940.

43. Shannon Development, *Bunratty castle and folk park brochure,* Shannon, 1991.

44. S. Popplewell (ed.), *The Irish museums guide,* Dublin, 1983.

45. L. Dodd, ' Sleeping with the past : collecting and Ireland,' *Circa* 59, Sept.-Oct. 1991, 29.

46. D. Lowenthal, *The past is a foreign country,* Cambridge, 1988.

47. University of Ulster, ' Talks & Tours ' 90,' *The Causeway coast* 12, 2, 1990, 24-5.

Some Guides to the Irish Scene